Ce

D0575245

Endangered
OCEAN ANIMALS

Marie Allgor

PowerKiDS
press

New York

Published in 2013 by The Rosen Publishing Group, Inc.
29 East 21st Street, New York, NY 10010

First Edition

Editor: Jennifer Way
Book Design: Julio Gil

Photo Credits: Cover, pp. 4, 5, 6, 7, 10, 11, 13 (inset), 16, 18, 22 Shutterstock.com; p. 5 (inset) Luis Javier Sandoval/Oxford Scientific/Getty Images; p. 8 © www.iStockphoto.com/Marshall Bruce; p. 9 Georgette Douwma/Photographer's Choice/Getty Images; p. 11 RFCD GeoAtlas; p. 12 Sue Flood/The Image Bank/Getty Images; p. 13 Richard Herrmann/Oxford Scientific/Getty Images; pp. 14–15 Danita Delimont/Gallo Images/Getty Images; p. 17 Oliver Grunewald/Oxford Scientific/Getty Images; p. 20 Mauricio Handler/National Geographic/Getty Images; p. 21 Lasting Images/Photolibrary/Getty Images.

Library of Congress Cataloging-in-Publication Data

Allgor, Marie.
Endangered ocean animals / By Marie Allgor. — 1st ed.
    p. cm. — (Save earth's animals!)
  Includes index.
  ISBN 978-1-4488-7420-0 (library binding) — ISBN 978-1-4488-7493-4 (pbk.) —
ISBN 978-1-4488-7567-2 (6-pack)
  1. Marine animals—Juvenile literature. 2. Endangered species—Juvenile literature. I. Title.
  QL122.2.A46 2013
  591.680914'2—dc23
                                2011046911

Manufactured in China

CPSIA Compliance Information: Batch # WKTS12PK: For Further Information contact Rosen Publishing, New York, New York at 1-800-237-9932

Contents

Welcome to the Ocean Biome!

Do you know what a **biome** is? It is a large community of plants and animals that live in the same major **habitat**. The world's largest biome is the ocean. It covers nearly three-quarters of Earth's surface. The ocean holds around 230,000 **species** that we know about. Scientists think there might

The sea otter lives in the northern and eastern Pacific Ocean. It is an endangered species.

The rainbow parrot fish lives in coral reefs in the Caribbean Sea and the Atlantic Ocean.

This is a great white shark. It lives in coastal waters throughout much of the world. There are more than 400 known species of sharks in Earth's oceans.

be 10 times that many species in the ocean that have yet to be found!

While it is true that the ocean is full of life, some species are in trouble. Due to **overfishing**, pollution, and **climate** change, animals such as the loggerhead sea turtle, the dugong, and the humpback whale are threatened or endangered.

Ocean Climates

It may seem odd to think of the ocean as having climates, but it does! Just as do climates on land, ocean climates differ based on where they are. Waters near the equator are warmer. Those that are far north or south are colder.

The ocean is warm in the Great Barrier Reef because it is near the equator and its depth is in the sunlit zone.

This humpback whale is swimming in the cold water off the coast of Antarctica.

Scientists break the ocean into zones to talk about how much sunlight it gets. The sunlit zone is shallow enough that it gets enough sunlight for plants to grow. Below that is the twilight zone. This zone gets less light, so plants do not grow there. The midnight zone is the deepest, darkest part of the ocean.

Ocean Habitats

Each of the ocean's zones is home to different kinds of animals. Some animals spend time in more than one zone. Crabs, fish, snails, and clams are a few of the animals that live in the sunlit zone. The twilight zone has squid, fish, and **plankton**. The midnight zone has some fish, **invertebrates**, and **bacteria** living there.

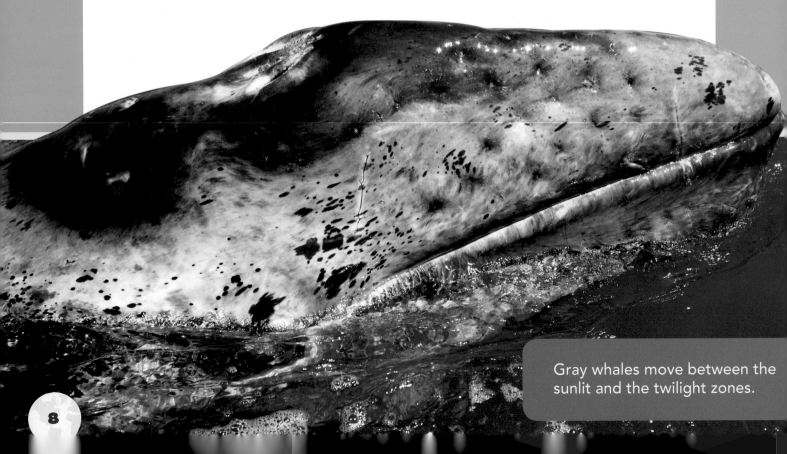

Gray whales move between the sunlit and the twilight zones.

8

Coral reefs are in the sunlit zone.

Coral reefs are special ocean habitats that are rich in plant and animal life. Generally in warm, shallow waters, these colorful habitats are home to so many living things. Colorful fish, sponges, sea anemones, sea dragons, dolphins, sharks, and many other animals live there.

The Ocean's Endangered Animals

There are more than 600 endangered species in Earth's oceans, and that number is growing larger. The animals on these pages are endangered and could one day become **extinct**.

MAP KEY

- Steller Sea Lion
- Blue Whale
- Southern Bluefin Tuna
- Leatherback Sea Turtle
- Ornate Eagle Ray

Leatherback
Sea Turtle

1. Southern Bluefin Tuna

Bluefin tuna have been fished for thousands of years. Today the southern bluefin tuna is critically endangered due to overfishing.

2. Ornate Eagle Ray

Ornate eagle rays are not seen very often, and sadly their numbers are dropping. They have become endangered due to fishing in the places where they live.

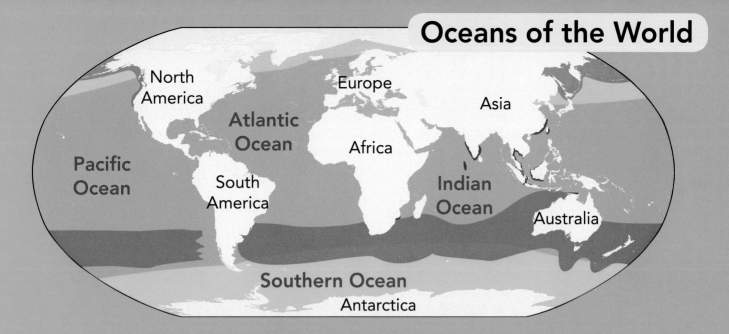

Oceans of the World

North America

Europe

Asia

Atlantic Ocean

Africa

Pacific Ocean

South America

Indian Ocean

Australia

Southern Ocean

Antarctica

3. Leatherback Sea Turtle

Leatherback sea turtles often return each year to the nesting grounds where they were born. Nesting-ground loss is one reason they are endangered. They also die from eating garbage that looks like their favorite food, jellyfish.

Steller Sea Lion

4. Steller Sea Lion

Between about 1970 and 2000, the population of Steller sea lions in northern seas dropped about 54 percent. The western population dropped about 70 percent during that time!

5. Blue Whale

The blue whale is Earth's largest animal. Blue whales were hunted almost to extinction. Today, laws protect these animals from hunters, but their numbers are still recovering.

Bluefin Tuna

Bluefin tuna are the largest tuna. There are three species. They are Atlantic, Pacific, and southern bluefin tuna. These fish can be up to 6.5 feet (2 m) and 550 pounds (250 kg)! They are valued and are often eaten raw as sushi. Overfishing has put Atlantic and southern bluefins on the endangered list.

Today laws are in place to help bluefin numbers grow while still letting fishermen catch some.

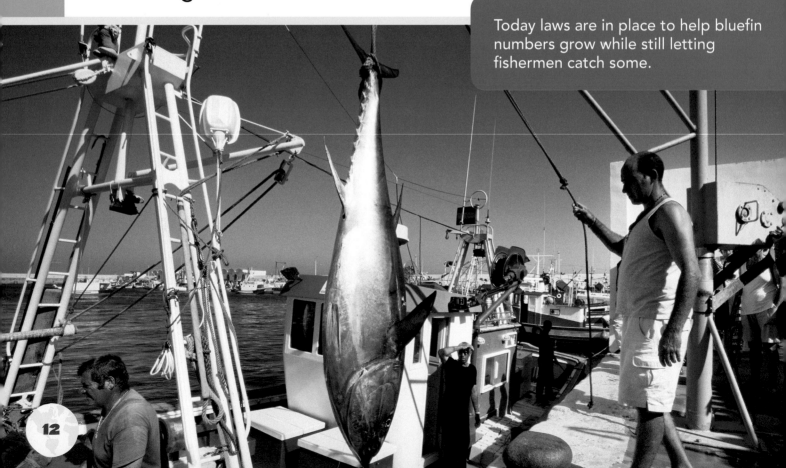

Built for swimming quickly over long distances, bluefin tuna can pull their dorsal and pectoral fins into slots in their bodies to lessen drag from the water.

Bluefin tuna eat smaller fish, such as mackerel, shown here.

Bluefin tuna can swim up to 43 miles per hour (70 km/h). They migrate huge distances several times a year. Atlantic bluefin have a special adaptation that most fish do not have. They are **warm-blooded**. This allows them to swim in both warm and cold waters.

Spotted Eagle Rays

The spotted eagle ray has a flat body with white spots. It grows to be 6 feet (1.8 m) across. It is found near coral reefs and on the shallow, sandy bottoms of the Atlantic Ocean, Pacific Ocean, and Indian Ocean. Spotted eagle rays eat a wide variety of crustaceans, mollusks, and some smaller fish.

Spotted eagle rays are listed as near threatened and will

Spotted eagle rays have white spots on their dark blue or black bodies. This ray is swimming near the Galápagos Islands, in the Pacific Ocean.

likely become endangered because their numbers are dropping due to the growth of fishing. They are not often fished themselves but are sometimes caught as bycatch. This means they are caught in nets meant for other fish.

Leatherback Sea Turtles

Leatherbacks are huge sea turtles. Unlike most other sea turtles, which have bony shells, the leatherback's shell is softer and more rubbery. They can grow to be 7 feet (2.1 m) long and weigh more than 2,000 pounds (900 kg). This makes them the largest sea turtles on Earth.

To lay their eggs, leatherbacks climb out of the water. They dig holes in the sand and lay their eggs inside. They then cover the nest and head back to the sea.

Here is a baby leatherback sea turtle just after it has hatched. Other animals will eat many leatherback hatchlings before they can reach the water!

Leatherbacks migrate a long way from the places where they eat to the places they have babies. The trip is about 3,700 miles (6,000 km) each way. Sadly, fishing, pollution, and loss of coastal nesting places have placed the leatherback on the endangered list.

Steller Sea Lions

Steller sea lions live in the cold waters off central California, Alaska, Canada, Japan, and Russia. These huge, noisy seals come together in large groups to **breed**. Males are about 10.5 feet (3.2 m) long and weigh more than 1,200 pounds (544 kg). Females are about 9 feet (2.7 m) long and weigh 580 pounds (263 kg).

Steller sea lions hunt close to the shore for fish, squid, and octopuses. While they are hunting, they must be on the lookout for orcas. Scientists also think that fishing has affected this sea lion's food supply, leading to its decline.

Steller sea lions are also called northern sea lions. These sea lions gather in groups on rocks near the coast.

Hector's Dolphins

Hector's dolphin is the world's smallest dolphin, growing to be just 5 feet (1.5 m) long. It is also one of the rarest dolphins in the world. Hector's dolphins do not start **mating** until they are between seven and nine years old. Females have just one calf every two to three years. This is one reason it takes their numbers so long to grow.

Hector's dolphins have gray bodies with black and white markings. There are only about 7,500 of these dolphins left in the world.

Because Hector's dolphins live close to shore, they can get hit by fishing boats or caught in fishing nets.

Hector's dolphins fish close to New Zealand's shore. The dolphins often get caught in fishermen's nets and die. Boats also hit and kill these dolphins. New Zealand's government is working hard to save these beautiful marine **mammals**.

Save Ocean Animals!

The ocean is home to so many amazing animals. Scientists are working to understand more about this huge biome and all the living things that call it home.

The scalloped hammerhead shark is endangered due to being caught for its fins, which are a special food in some countries.

Overfishing and pollution are two problems facing ocean animals. Laws have been passed worldwide to limit how many animals are fished each year. Organizations such as Greenpeace work to bring attention to issues that affect animals and the environment. Hopefully, these efforts will help endangered ocean animals.

Glossary

BACTERIA (bak-TIR-ee-uh) Tiny living things that cannot be seen with the eye alone.

BIOME (BY-ohm) A kind of place with certain weather patterns and kinds of plants.

BREED (BREED) To make babies.

CLIMATE (KLY-mut) The kind of weather a certain place has.

EXTINCT (ik-STINGKT) No longer existing.

HABITAT (HA-buh-tat) The kind of land where an animal or a plant naturally lives.

INVERTEBRATES (in-VER-teh-brets) Animals without backbones.

MAMMALS (MA-mulz) Warm-blooded animals that have backbones and hair, breathe air, and feed milk to their young.

MATING (MAYT-ing) Coming together to make babies.

OVERFISHING (oh-ver-FISH-ing) Catching too many fish.

PLANKTON (PLANK-ten) Tiny plants and animals that drift with water currents.

SPECIES (SPEE-sheez) One kind of living thing. All people are one species.

WARM-BLOODED (WORM-bluh-did) Having a body heat that stays the same, no matter how warm or cold the surroundings are.

Index

Websites

Due to the changing nature of Internet links, PowerKids Press has developed an online list of websites related to the subject of this book. This site is updated regularly. Please use this link to access the list: www.powerkidslinks.com/sea/ocean/